Objections! Objections! Objections!

Published 2004

ISBN 1-84294-127-5

Layout: Stephen ML Young
stephenmlyoung@aol.com

Printed and bound by Digisource (GB) Limited

Objections! Objections! Objections!

How to Conquer Objections and Explode Your Sales Performance!

By Gavin Ingham

Acknowledgements

Hello and thank you for buying **Objections! Objections! Objections!** In this book my aim is to help you to dramatically improve your ability to handle objections both when selling and in your life in general.

In today's frenetic business environment most books go unread, their learning unimplemented. With this in mind, I have designed a book that can be read from cover to cover quickly, dipped into at leisure, referred to as a resource, added to for personalisation or merely assimilated a few pages at a time.

As a child I had a favourite picture which, at first glance, was easy on the eye and fun to look at yet the more that you looked at its simplicity the more depth there was behind it. This book is modelled on that memory and will provide you with new ideas, strategies and distinctions each and every time that you choose to explore its pages. Whether you're a seasoned sales professional, you're just starting out in sales or you're a business person looking to improve your communications you will find something of value within these pages.

Many sales books talk about objections and objection handling but then fail to put their money where their mouth is and produce a truly useable guide that salespeople everywhere will want to keep on their desks. This is truly achieved in **Objections! Objections! Objections!**

I know that you will benefit from this book and that it will form a powerful and effective backbone for your sales career. I hope to meet you at one of my seminars, keynotes or programmes one day but in the meantime go out and sell with attitude!

Gavin

Testimonials

"I really enjoyed the seminar and learnt more about cold calling in one day than I have done in the last 5 years!"

Danielle Pile, Roevin

"Friday's seminar was excellent. I don't think I have ever been on a course where I haven't lost interest along the way. Gavin kept it interesting and upbeat (so much energy!)."

Sarah Bradshaw, Capita

"I was blown away by the quality and content of your "Power Canvassing" seminar that I found very entertaining as well as informative. Where as some training I have attended in the past has died on its feet in a few days, the tools and techniques that I learnt on Power Canvassing are still ringing in my ears. Gavin's enthusiasm is contagious and his knowledge prodigious. With a combination of "Real World" tools and techniques that get results, I feel that every recruitment consultancy that is interested in exploding their consultants motivation and sales figures would benefit from your seminars".

Simon Childs BSc (Hons), Senior Consultant, Chase Moulande Regeneration

"I recently attended Power Canvassing seminar and must say it was quite different to other 'sales' courses I have been on. I found Gavin Ingham very motivational. Most sales courses will tell you about objection handling but the difference ......is that they go a lot deeper than that. How you actually feel before you make the call is very

important. You have to recognise that the sales call is 100% your responsibility so when things don't go according to plan take the time to learn from your mistakes – could you have handled the call better. If not, the most important thing is to let that call go and move on .... shows you how to do this by changing your attitude and physiological state, continually practising and asking for feedback from colleagues. I will definitely be recommending (Gavin) ... to my colleagues!"

Edith Udemezue, Operations manager, Science Recruitment Group

"Yesterday was a highly energised day with lots of ideas and audience participation. I was able to take away a lot of re-enforced traits and some new approaches for overcoming the many obstacles that are put in our way on a daily basis."

Iain Brassell, TMP Worldwide

"It was excellent, I have learnt a lot about how we can expand the mind.... Thoroughly enjoyed my day. The trainer was superb and the whole day was very beneficial. I feel very motivated, hope it lasts!!!"

Kelly Duffield, The Recruitment Consultant Magazine

"Interesting, informative and fun. Good trainer. Kept us interested and at our level."

Justine Wilkinson, Training Manager, Preferred International

Who is Gavin Ingham?

Gavin is the foremost sales performance expert in the UK. He passionately believes in helping individuals and teams create the lives and businesses that they desire. With his inspirational approach to sales and motivation Gavin combines commercial experience, personal excellence and communications technologies in delivering personal and business sales success.

Unlike many so called experts, Gavin excelled as a sales professional winning a European sales award for a leading organisation in his first year of selling and then progressed rapidly through to a hands-on managerial role. After a successful start-up project, he worked as Head of Sales and Marketing in a FTSE 250 before setting up his own business helping others to rapidly increase their personal and business sales success.

Gavin is an NLP Master Practitioner, CIPD qualified and a trained coach. His depth of sales and commercial experience allows him to share true-life anecdotes and examples, which resonate with audiences. This shared experience encourages greater learning and application of the skills taught because the salespeople know that Gavin understands them. Gavin believes that it's important that every investment produces real results and that is his primary objective when working with clients.

Lifelong learning and the application of that learning is the key to all success. Gavin is committed to studying, modelling and working with the best in his key areas of study. These include sales, coaching, communications and NLP. Gavin particularly enjoys the works of Anthony Robbins, Brian Tracy, Stephen Covey, Steve Andreas, Robert Dilts, Milton Erickson and Richard Bandler.

Gavin is the creator of the Power Canvassing seminars, CD's and various other audio products. He also created a phenomenal 12-week programme methodology designed to produce sustainable sales growth and return on investment.

During his career Gavin has won business with a multitude of blue-chip clients including IBM, Lloyds TSB, AT&T, Siemens, Vodafone and Citibank and has trained and coached successful sales teams, sales professionals, managers and business owners.

Gavin's Philosophy

"Whatever your sport you wouldn't play without the guidance and support of an experienced coach on your side. The same should be true of your business. After all, your business is the most important game there is.

That's why my dynamic programmes are so important. This unique combination of consultancy, training and coaching serves sales professionals, business owners, and dynamic teams in their desire to create more sales and stronger businesses."

Objections! Objections! Objections!

How to Conquer Objections and Explode Your Sales Performance!

By Gavin Ingham

Contents

How to Use this Book

Do...

- Personalise it by adding your own answers, comments, scribbles and drawings
- Read it from cover to cover
- Dip into it whenever you have a spare moment
- Keep it on your desk or in your briefcase
- Note your sales "wins" within its pages
- Memorise your favourite answers
- Find yourself adopting the beliefs and living the life of a Sales Superstar
- Use it as a resource for creative 10 minute energisers in sales meetings and trainings
- Buy copies for the whole of your sales team
- Tell your friends about it
- Use it as the secret of your success!

Top 10 Tips of Sales Superstars

1 No objection has any meaning other than the meaning which you give to it

2 Always be 100% responsible for the outcome of every client interaction

3 Always remain calm in the face of client objections

4 No-one has the power to make you feel bad unless you let them

5 Dealing with objections is simply part of selling

6 Dealing with objections expertly will set you apart from mere average salespeople

7 Modelling successful salespeople and studying books and audio products is part of being at the top of your game

8 Write down every objection you can think of, plan your answers and practice them until you are fluent in the use of them

9 Constantly revise and improve your objection handling techniques

10 Believe in yourself, your product / service and the sales profession

When You Become an Expert Objection Handler...

You will:

- Build better rapport with clients
- Stay more focused on your sales objectives
- Remain on calls longer
- Be less stressed
- Feel great about your chosen profession
- Enjoy the sales process much more
- Avoid confrontation with clients
- Be more persuasive
- Become a master of communicating in difficult situations
- Portray professionalism, confidence and client focus
- Prevent most objections ever happening!
- Make more sales at higher fees!

And in the Beginning there was Feel, Felt, Found

FEEL I understand the way that you feel
FELT Other people felt that way too!
FOUND However, what they found was ... Answer objection!

Strengths

- Easy to use and remember
- Adaptable

Weaknesses

- No good for complaints or personal objections (e.g. *"I don't like you!"*)
- Can't be used over and over for multiple objections

Sales Superstar says...

"Consider your most common objections and plan and personalise your Feel / Felt / Found answers with real life examples and statistics."

"I understand how you feel John. When I worked with *(name client)* ***they felt that the initial investment was outside of their budget too. After implementing Gavin's coaching programmes across their organisation they found that their sales rose by 45% which represents a 275% return on investment. This equates to a bottom line profit figure of ...*** *(name figure)****."***

Practise now!

Top 10 Tips for Dealing with Objections

1. Take your time
2. Clarify the objection
3. Don't waffle
4. Choose your words carefully
5. Take a deep breath
6. Watch the pace of your speech
7. Listen! Listen! Listen!
8. Answer the right objection
9. Ask a question
10. Remember that you cannot lose what you haven't got!

Voice Coaching and Making an Impact

Control of the voice and its qualities is outside of most people's conscious awareness most of the time. For this reason it is an area of study that gets little attention in most sales training. This is unfortunate because, as we all know, it's not what you say it's the way that you say it. It's therefore essential that you master this important sales and life skill.

Pace. Keep your pace steady and controlled. This shows professionalism and seniority sending the message that you are listening and that you are considering what the client has to say! Ironically, most of us have a tendency under pressure to rush, which sends completely the opposite message.

Tone is simply the expression of feelings in your voice i.e. confident, happy, knowledgeable, dynamic etc. Consider how you want to come over on your calls. The component parts of your tone should be flexible to each and every client and each and every situation. The way to convey a tone is to "do" the feeling.

Pitch is the note that your voice is on – high or low. This is particularly useful in relationship to the ends of sentences. Try saying out loud, *"You've probably heard of us"* but concentrate on keeping a level pitch at the end of the sentence. As you listen to it you will hear that this is a statement. Now try the same statement but going down at the end of the sentence. You will hear that this is an order. Now try going up at the end of the sentence. This sounds like a question.

Many salespeople go up under pressure and invite objections by sounding like they are asking a question! Conversely, using the downward or order tone can be incredibly powerful for controlling conversations.

Practice. Whilst all of this sounds very simple; in practice you will have habitual patterns of speech that you may find very difficult to change. It can also be very difficult to even identify your own voice patterns as you often don't hear yourself the same way as everyone else does. I would highly recommend getting others to listen to and critique your calls, focusing on these elements that we have discussed.

Judge by results. Because the non-verbal elements of the call are mostly outside of conscious awareness this means that when you do perfect these skills you will add that magical element to your answers. This will increase not only your sales results but also your ability to build rapport with your clients.

For more on this subject why not listen to one of my audio products or attend one of my seminars.

The Objections!

"I don't know your company."

What client means

"Who are you?"
Clients have found that purely "emotional" objections like this one quickly uncover the insecurities of average salespeople.

Average salesperson

Thinks: *"No you don't. Why does no-one like me?"*
Action: Becomes defensive, waffles and ultimately bails out of the call.

"Fantastic! That's exactly why I've called. We're the *... (give opening statement or unique selling points)."*

Sales Superstar

Thinks: *"You will in a minute!"*
Understands: Peak performers are motivated from the inside out. Only average sales people are affected by this kind of comment.

Why this works

- It reframes the client's expectations of how salespeople behave
- It's positive and amusing
- It was never a real objection anyway!

"We don't use that!"

What client means

"I see no need for your services."
This client either does not see the need for your services or is using this approach as an instant conversation terminator.

Average salesperson

Thinks: *"No-one wants our products!"*
Action: Either bails out of the call or gets confrontational and pushes against the client's resistance.

"And I'm not asking you to change now, merely get to know you and understand a little more about your business and what you do use."

Sales Superstar

Thinks: *"And I'll find a need for it if you have one!"*
Understands: The parable of the two shoe salespeople in Africa. One messages back, *"Bring me home, no-one wears shoes out here"*, the other messages back, *"Send more shoes! No-one wears shoes out here!"*

Why this works

- Defuses "threat" of the pushy salesperson
- "Change now" is an embedded command
- Who doesn't like to talk about themselves and their business?

"All of that is controlled by head office in the USA."

What client means

"It's not in my control."
Client does not want to waste time talking about something that is not within his control. It's also a great way of getting rid of unwanted salespeople!

Average salesperson

Thinks: "Why is nothing as easy as it used to be?"
Action: Bails out of the call and adds to their collection of negative sales memories.

"Where in the US?
Who looks after it?
What's his / her role?
What's their phone number?
When was that implemented?

(And gradually move into...)

How effective has it been?
What were the business reasons for implementing that in the first place?"

Sales Superstar

Thinks: *"You can't stop me that easily!"*
Understands: Building business relationships in today's markets is like putting together the many pieces of a complex puzzle. Only by building many lines of communication can the picture be completed.

Why this works

- Uses "misdirection" to gather information and lets client think that you're asking standard sales questions. This helps them to relax and allows you to build deeper rapport
- You then move to deeper questions so that you can uncover needs and opportunities

"I'm afraid that area of the business is outsourced."

What client means

"Not today!"
In today's markets, outsourcing areas of the business is becoming increasingly popular with companies seeking to reduce overheads, cut costs and maximise profits. Ordinary salespeople are too focused on products and not commercially minded enough to understand the potential opportunities here.

Average salesperson

Thinks: *"I could have been somebody! This market is rubbish!"*
Action: Thanks client and departs with another notch on their *"woe is me"* belt.

"That's fine. As someone focused on providing specialist solutions in that area I'm pleased that you take it so seriously. I'm curious, what were your reasons for outsourcing that area of your business in the first place?"

Sales Superstar

Thinks: *"We'll see about that!"*
Understands: As fast as one area is outsourced another is brought back in-house. Careful investigation may uncover alternative opportunities, "middle-man" deals and even problems in the existing outsourcing solution.

Why this works

- Positions you as an expert
- Respects client's position
- *"I'm curious"* is a real "softener"
- Links nicely to questions

"I haven't enough time."

What client means

"I'm busy and you'd better not waste my time." This kind of objection usually means that the client is busy and that they get a lot of sales calls. It's really not personal but most salespeople take it this way!

Average salesperson

Thinks: *"I'll be as quick as possible then!"*
Action: Makes excuses for the call, rushes into the pitch and gets rejected. When salespeople rush in this way it sends a psychological message that they are not important and therefore not worth dealing with.

Attempt 1:
"And I won't waste a moment of your time."

Attempt 2 (if he repeats himself):
***"I apologise. When this week would be more convenient to call?
How would Friday afternoon be for you? 3 or 4pm?"***

(Book call or meeting)

Sales Superstar

Thinks: *"I am worthy of your time."*
Understands: All clients make time for the right sales conversations therefore the key here is to maintain composure and differentiate your call as being worthy of the client's time. Ensure that you control your pace, tone and pitch.

Why this works

- The initial acknowledgement is enough for most clients
- Takes responsibility if the client repeats the objection
- Sets a time for the conversation using different closing techniques

"You're too expensive!"

What client means

"I reckon I can get a bargain here."
The "price" objection is one of the most feared by salespeople and clients know it! What's more they are not afraid to use it liberally.

Average salesperson

Thinks: *"Quick! Give him a discount – I'm too expensive!"*
Action: Reduces price, appears desperate, throws away an opportunity.

Option 1: ***"I'm sure you have a good reason for saying that, do you mind me asking you what it is?"***

Option 2: ***"Are you considering the price or the total cost of ownership? Certainly when you look at the price on a piece of paper we're not the cheapest. When you consider the total cost of ownership which includes ...*** *(name client's needs / criteria)* ***... then you will be able to see that we provide the best return on investment."***

Option 3: ***"Well, I certainly don't mind people selling for less. However, and you will understand why I ask you this, how important is it that any purchase provides a return on investment? Why? And you know that's exactly why..."***

Sales Superstar

Thinks: *"You've just not understood the value yet!"*
Understands: Clients are always going to try and negotiate and most aren't that serious about it anyway. If they are the Sales Superstar will ask questions to build the value before negotiating.

Why this works

- Shows empathy
- Uncovers real costs not just figures
- Reframes the client's perspective
- Shows confidence and professionalism

"I'm happy with my current suppliers thank you."

What client means

"I get these calls all of the time."
Clients have found that most sales people have no useful answer to this objection! They often use it without any consideration as to whether they really are happy or not.

Average salesperson

Thinks: *"Everyone has a supplier already! Why do I bother with this job?"*
Action: Bails out of the call or challenges for a weakness in the client's existing relationships. This usually results in confrontation.

Attempt 1:
"Great and I'm not asking you to change now merely consider building a relationship..."

Attempt 2:
"Many of my other clients told me the same thing. They were also working with existing suppliers before they realised that our service perfectly complemented what they were already doing. I'd like to get together and show you how..."

Sales Superstar

Thinks: *"Really! We'll see about that!"*
Understands: It has been estimated that only 5% of clients are genuinely "happy" with their current suppliers but most won't tell you until you've got significant amounts of trust and rapport.

Why this works

- Does not challenge or threaten the existing supplier relationship
- Respects the client's decision
- *"Change now"* is an embedded command
- Uses inclusive approach with the word *"complemented"*

"We've got a preferred supplier's list!"

What client means

"Not today thank you!"
In some industries this objection is the most feared objection that there is. Clients know this and produce it with a flourish leaving a trail of battered salespeople in their wake!

Average salesperson

Thinks: *"Not again! I hate this job!"*
Action: Asks when the list is up for renewal, sends some literature and books a call-back for some "more appropriate" time in the future.

"I'm pleased to hear that! Many of our partner companies have preferred supplier's lists as well. I'm sure that you had good business reasons for setting that up. Do you mind telling me, what were they?"

Sales Superstar

Thinks: *"And I know that you don't always use it!"*
Understands: Clients virtually always source some services / products outside of their existing supplier relationships. Getting onto the list requires a long-term strategy so there are two different angles here – one for the short-term and one for the long-term.

Why this works

- Acknowledges client's position
- Reframes salesperson's position as a partner
- Links to information seeking questions

"We're about to be taken over."

What client means

"I'm in trouble and this is bad timing."
This client may be feeling very vulnerable right now. He won't be wanting to speak with brash sales people.

Average salesperson

Thinks: *"There by the grace of God go I!"*
Action: Feels embarrassed, sees no opportunity, exits the call or (far worse) pushes to try to expose needs right now in a very unsubtle manner!

"I'm sorry to hear that, those situations are always challenging …
(move to questions about the take over)."

Sales Superstar

Thinks: *"Poor chap. Maybe I can help."*
Understands: Measured empathy can go a long way right now. In the future this client may end up being promoted in the turmoil or may even end up winning a more influential position elsewhere.

Why this works

- Shows professional empathy and builds rapport
- *"Those"* linguistically distances both of you from the situation slightly
- Moving to questions builds rapport
- Allows you to judge the next step carefully

"We're making redundancies at the moment."

What client means

"Have you no sensitivity?"
This client is either worrying about his own job or is buried in the middle of a very difficult management scenario. A pushy, proactive salesperson talking about opportunities and requirements is not on his agenda!

Average salesperson

Thinks: *"I can't believe it. What a waste of my time!"*
Action: Gives up, feels bad, takes a step closer to another wasted day in the office!

"I'm sorry to hear that – it's never easy to make business decisions like that. When you consider the importance of any strategic decision like that it is essential to have the right support systems in place. It may be that we can help, tell me..."

Sales Superstar

Thinks: *"I wonder what opportunities may lie within those business challenges?"*
Understands: Companies always have business reasons for making decisions like this whether due to increased technology or difficult market conditions. Maybe the Sales Superstar can provide a solution to one of the problems. In any case, most companies expand again at some point.

Why this works

- Empathises with client's situation
- Demonstrates strategic business awareness
- Reframes client perspective from problems to solutions and moves into any question that you believe appropriate

"It's the end of the financial year at the moment. We can't look at anything until the new financial year."

What client means

"I'm really busy. Go away."
This objection could well be the truth or it could well be a fabrication. In any case, this client is using an objection which works wonders on most salespeople. The client just knows how they are going to respond!

Average salesperson

Thinks: *"Great! He's interested! I'll call back in the new financial year!"*
Action: Asks when the new financial year begins and books a call back into his database for then. Sadly, you could spend whole sales careers ringing back clients like this one with little chance of a deal.

***"That's good news because I wasn't wanting to show you anything right now just introduce myself and gain a greater understanding of you and your business. Tell me** ... (move to questions)."*

Sales Superstar

Thinks: *"Oh really! Let's see what we can do about that!"*
Understands: Business doesn't stop for 3 months prior to the end of the financial year like many clients claim. If the client can't see any value in you and your proposition right now why will he be able to do so in 3 months time? More information is needed from the client.

Why this works

- Reframes client's expectations with the opening statement
- *"Because"* creates a subconscious link to a totally reasonable objective of introducing yourself
- *"You and your"* shows interest in the client

"I've got no budget."

Client means

"I've got no budget for you."
Clients know that 95% of salespeople will ask when they do have a budget and arrange to call them back then. What a great way of getting rid of salespeople!

Average salesperson

Thinks: *"This job is rubbish, the market's rubbish; no-one ever has any budget."*
Action: Becomes disconsolate, fails to build rapport and creates a weak pipeline.

"Thanks for sharing that with me. When I first spoke to them many of my clients didn't have budgets and that's what makes us different. At this point most companies would probably ask when you do have a budget and not talk now. We at ... *(name company)* ***... believe in building strong relationships with our clients and I'd like to invest in getting to know you now."***

Sales Superstar

Thinks: *"Not yet you haven't."*
Understands: Most salespeople will bail out of this call here so this is a great opportunity to build a relationship and win a client that others have ignored. Also, most clients can create or reallocate budgets if they perceive a big enough need.

Why this works

- Acknowledges client's situation
- Uses a 3rd party experience to reframe the situation
- *"Talk now"* is an embedded command
- *"Invest in"* the client is flattering

"Is this a sales call?"

What client means

"Are you a waste of space?"
Many clients get dozens of calls a day from unprofessional salespeople from which they develop beliefs and perceptions about the value of salespeople in society. Giving salespeople a hard time can (at some level) also make clients feel better about themselves!

Average salesperson

Thinks: *"Oh no! I've been sussed again! If only I'd have worked harder at school!"*
Action: Makes excuses, talks too quickly, appears unconfident and, unsurprisingly, gets rejected.

"Yes / No / or Well ... *(you choose which!)*
The reason for my call is to introduce myself and my company..."

Sales Superstar

Thinks: *"You'd better believe it!"*
Understands: Dealing with other people's insecurities is part of the role of a sales professional. No one can detract from the Sales Superstar's belief that he provides a valuable service to his clients.

Why this works

- Answers the question!
- Takes control in a professional manner
- Implies the importance of the call via the style of the delivery

"I've got no need."

What client means

"No thanks!"
Logically, this is the most obvious of objections but it is not used as much as it might be by clients because of its somewhat direct nature. As such, if it is used it is usually by fairly direct clients who like to get to the point, fast!

Average salesperson

Thinks: *"Another one! Why is it that no-one has any need for me?"*
Action: Gives up and exits the call or tries to convince the client that they either do have a need or that they would have one if they knew how great the salesperson's solution / product was. Either option equals resistance.

"And I'm not asking you to buy now John, merely keep your self appraised of opportunities available in the market right now. Tell me John..."

Sales Superstar

Thinks: *"At last! An opportunity worthy of my sales abilities!"*
Understands: The vast majority of salespeople are "order-takers" dealing only with clients who are well advanced in the sales process. Sales Superstars help their clients to implement solutions which will help their businesses now and in the future.

Why this works

- Avoids pushing against a "closed door"
- Is full of embedded commands – *"buy now"*, *"keep yourself appraised"* and *"right now"*
- Links to questions

"I don't want whatever it is!"

Client means

"I'm busy and I've had a lot of calls lately."
This client is exasperated with the numbers of calls that they are getting. This all-encompassing blanket objection is designed to terminate any and all sales calls as fast as possible.

Average salesperson

Thinks: *"Not surprised! No-one ever does!"*
Action: Puts on his "sales" hat and tries to "sell" the client on his product. At best this will result in a swift exit from the call!!

"And I certainly won't try to sell anything to you now. The reason for my call is to introduce myself and my company..."

Sales Superstar

Thinks: *"Lets rock 'n 'roll!"*
Understands: This client has to make their purchases somewhere and with an approach like that most salespeople will have fallen at the first hurdle. Its time for the Sales Superstar to make their move!

Why this works

- It's not much of an objection really so it will more than likely just go away once you don't rise to the bait!
- Links back to relationship building

"Just give me the price."

What client means

"Get it over with and I can tell you to go away." This client is taking control and trying to rush the salesperson to the point where they can reject them. Most salespeople will just give the price and leave the client to their own decision making process.

Average salesperson

Thinks: *"Here comes a price rejection and we'll be too expensive."*
Action: Gives the price in a very defensive and unconfident manner, precipitates a price objection and fails to win the sale.

"I certainly will do. However, as you would expect there are various different solutions available. In order to make sure that you get the best return on investment and the right solution I need to ask you some questions. From that I'll give you the best price. Tell me John... "

Sales Superstar

Thinks: "*Woah there boy! Not until I've established a big enough need!*"
Understands: Average salespeople invite their own objections by quoting prices too early in the sales process. Sales Superstars deal with potential objections before they surface. They ensure that the client has a strong need prior to talking figures.

Why this works

- Agrees with request
- Everyone wants the "*best price*"
- Reframes price as "*investment*"
- Links to questions about the business

"We don't take cold calls."

What client means

"We're too important to talk to you!"
In an effort to reduce time wasting and increase profitability some companies have introduced clearly unenforceable policies such as this. Despite the ambiguity of this comment, it's more than enough of an obstacle for most salespeople.

Average salesperson

Thinks: *"And that's what I do isn't it! What a useless job!"*
Action: Exits call, argues or becomes desperate. Not good!

"That's fine because the reason for my call is to introduce myself and my company..."

Sales Superstar

Thinks: *"You just did!"*
Understands: Selling is a serious profession that provides unrivalled career opportunities to the best players. Cold calling plays an important part in the Sales Superstar's toolkit.

Why this works

- None confrontational
- Agrees with client then links with word *"because"* to a reframing of the client's perspective about the call

"Haven't you anything better to do?"

What client means

"I'm having a bad day and I'm taking it out on you!"
This put down is a deliberate blow aimed at the salesperson's confidence. It's likely to come from clients who are having a bad day and is very effective in getting rid of sales people.

Average salesperson

Thinks: *"No."*
Action: Feels really bad about themselves and then becomes really defensive about their role and their job. Usually gabbles a lot!

Option 1:
Totally ignore the objection all together and carry on with the call. **"Actually the reason for the call..."**

Option 2:
"That's a very philosophical question and one which I'll happily discuss another time. The reason for my call today is..."

Sales Superstar

Thinks: *"What could be better than selling?"*
Understands: A Sales Superstar is 100% responsible for managing their own internal state irrespective of the actions of anyone around them. A meaningless question like this will not effect them in any way whatsoever.

Why this works

- This objection deserves little airtime
- 2nd option is humorous yet makes a serious point
- Respects client's position and gets to the point

"Look! There's a war on!"

(Or similar)

What client means

"Go away."
If your client intends to remain in business then they must purchase things to be able to run their business. This is either an excuse or a failure to realise the consequences of not continuing to invest in their business.

Average salesperson

Thinks: *"You don't have to tell me. I'm the one selling nothing."*
Action: Becomes apologetic or desperate.

"I know! That's exactly why I've called. When the market's picked up and we look back at this moment we'll know what a great time it is to build relationships and partnerships for the future."

Sales Superstar

Thinks: *"And?"*
Understands: Sales Superstars help clients to understand and develop their businesses by providing solutions to existing and future problems. Most clients need just as much (if not more) help in a difficult market.

Why this works

- Starts with a surprise agreement
- Uses time distortion to bring the current market problems into perspective
- Aligns client and salesperson together verbally

"Are you trying to sell me something?"

What client means

"Here we go! Another pushy sales pitch!"
This type of emotional objection has no real substance and is purely designed to make you feel bad. It could be the result of the client having a bad day, a bad experience or having deep-rooted psychological problems! In any case, it usually does the trick and gets rid of the salesperson.

Average salesperson

Thinks: *"Yes, I am and I know that I'm just a salesperson! Please don't rub it in!"*
Action: Uncovers the salesperson's personal insecurities causing them to become defensive.

"Yes / no / or well ... the reason for this call is to..."

Sales Superstar

Thinks: *"Not yet! But I will!"*
Understands: Most emotional objections simply disappear when the sales person demonstrates that they have no impact. Controlled pace, clarity and authority are important in the delivery of this reply.

Why this works

- Personal choice of answers
- All answer the client's question
- Sales Superstar remains unemotional and professional

"I've heard bad things about your company / product."

What client means

"I'm not sure about you."
Today's markets move very quickly and news travels very rapidly. Whether real or unreal, fact or fiction clients will often think that they have heard something negative about your company.

Average salesperson

Thinks: *"Not another one. How have we upset so many people?"*
Action: Starts to explain either how good the company is now or how things have changed within the company. The first option is too pushy and the second is likely to create more objections!

"I'm sorry to hear that, we certainly pride ourselves on our unrivalled reputation. Tell me *(name client)*, ***what have you heard?*** *(Listen!)*

I'm sorry about that, how would you like me to resolve this now so that we can move things forward?"

Sales Superstar

Thinks: *"I'm sure that I can help you to feel good about working with us!"*
Understands:
1) This is probably going to be a misunderstanding.
2) Some statistics show that 90%+ of complainants simply want to be listened to and to receive an apology.

Why this works

- Takes personal responsibility with the apology
- Listens to what happened
- Moves to a resolution *"now"* and understands that 90%+ of clients don't want anything more than the apology

"This is my 20th call today!"

What client means

"Don't waste my time."
This client is probably busy and doesn't want to waste time with irrelevant sales calls.

Average salesperson

Thinks: *"Oh dear! I'm a beggar!"*
Action: Rushing, unconfident, and apologetic the average performer quickly loses momentum and fails again!

Attempt 1:
"Well, I won't waste a moment of your time..."

Attempt 2:
"You know and that's exactly why I'm calling. It's not always convenient to take those types of calls. One of the things that we have done for partners is help to reduce them. In order to help to do that I need to..."

Sales Superstar

Thinks: *"And it might be your lucky day!"*
Understands: People run repetitive and habitual patterns of behaviour and this client needs their pattern interrupting!

Why this works

- Attempt 1 side-steps the objection
- Attempt 2 understands the client's perspective
- *"Those"* linguistically distinguishes you from the 20 calls
- Links to your next steps

"Go away!"
(Or worse!)

What client means

"Go away! I'm busy."
Objections like this one are reasonably rare although they do occur from time to time. As a rule most people are basically polite and this kind of objection usually manages to incense average salespeople.

Average salesperson

Thinks: *"How rude! Why do I have to be spoken to like this?"*
Action: Either exits the call fast or becomes confrontational. Not a great starting point for a relationship. Contrary to what most salespeople say, venting their emotions does not normally lead to a more resourceful state afterwards either!

"I certainly can do** (name client) **although there are several key factors prevalent in the market at the moment that could well be of interest to you. Tell me, how important is it to stay abreast of what's going on in the market right now?"

Sales Superstar

Thinks: *"Curious! I wonder what upset him?"*
Understands: Nothing has any meaning other than the meaning that we give to it therefore the Sales Superstar knows that he can choose how to interpret any situation. It may not be possible to deal with this client right now but the Sales Superstar is going to have a good try!

Why this works

- 1st try politely reframes client's experience
- 2nd try offers a "carrot" then moves to a question which it is hard to answer in the negative
- Using client's name makes it psychologically more difficult for them to be difficult again

"We've just bought one of those."

What client means

"We already have a supplier so we have no need." People often do look at things in black and white terms such as right versus wrong, up versus down and need versus no need. In any case, this simple objection gets rid of 90%+ of salespeople.

Average salesperson

Thinks: *"No-one ever needs me. How come I'm never lucky?"*
Action: Leaves call a loser or fights with the client about the validity of their recent purchase. Would you listen to someone who doesn't know you and your business telling you that you've not made the best decision?

"I'm sorry we weren't there to help that time. The reason for my call was actually to..."

Sales Superstar

Thinks: *"Great! So my information about you being a potential client was right!"*
Understands: Pushing against a closed door now would be foolish. All clients at some point assess the solution that they have implemented, the logistics of that purchase and the impact of any changes. Building a relationship now puts our Sales Superstar in pole position when doubt or future need comes along.

Why this works

- Takes responsibility
- *"That time"* puts the event into the past and moves the conversation forwards
- If the client objects again it will more than likely be a different objection e.g. no need.

"Does he know what the call's regarding?"

What client means

"I think that you're a salesperson."
Something has identified you as a salesperson and this person's role is to block sales calls. For most salespeople, gatekeepers are a major problem in their ability to get through to decision-makers. This is good news for clients who are trying to avoid sales calls and bad news for salespeople who want to make new contacts!

Average salesperson

Thinks: *"Oh no! Not this again!"*
Action: Gets confrontational!

"My name is Gavin, Gavin Ingham, the leading supplier of sales motivation in the UK. I work with senior managers to help them to increase turnover and maximise profitability in the sales arena. As you know, there are various competitive factors prevalent in the market at the moment that *(name client)* ***will be strategically aware of. If you could just let him know that I'm on the line. Thank you."***

Sales Superstar

Thinks: *"It's only a question and how I answer it will dictate my success."*
Understands: A change of tack is necessary here to differentiate the importance of your call. It's also worth looking at your opening statement if this is occurring frequently as something that you are doing is probably inviting this reaction from gatekeepers.

Why this works

- Implies first name terms
- Strategic element suggests seniority
- *"As you know"* is inclusive of the "blocker"
- Final line is a polite order
- "Blocker" wouldn't want to not put through someone that they should be putting through!

"Can I say who's calling?"

What client means

"Is this a sales call?"
Client believes that this is a sales call and is looking for confirmation in order to end the call. Much like the last scenario this innocent question is the beginning of a nightmare for many salespeople!

Average salesperson

Thinks: *"Busted!"*
Action: Approaches this question with a poor attitude and low in confidence. This usually ends in an equally dismal outcome!

"Yes, of course. If you could just let him know that it's Gavin, Gavin Ingham on the line for him. Thank you."

Sales Superstar

Thinks: *"I'm not falling for that!"*
Understands: "Blockers" are only doing their job and they will put through the calls that they need to! Belief, confidence and voice coaching all play a major part in dealing with gatekeepers successfully.

Why this works

- Answers question politely but firmly
- Minimises the request with a polite order
- Implies first name terms

"Speak to my PA."

What client means

"I'm too important to speak to you."
Clients habitually pass sales calls on to personal assistants because they don't see the value in having the conversation themselves. As an objection this works because many salespeople are relieved that they don't have to speak with a director!

Average salesperson

Thinks: *"No-one wants to speak with me and now I'm going to have to fight with the PA!"*
Action: Accepts this ploy and then gets into a power struggle with the PA.

"Thanks, I certainly can do. I work with senior decision makers like yourself and I specifically rang today to meet you. My name's Gavin Ingham and my company is the premier sales motivation company in the UK..."

Sales Superstar

Thinks: *"You must be joking!"*
Understands: Building relationships with PA's is and can be vital to the success of a sale but this is not the time. At best the PA will listen and make a decision, at worst reject you. This call needs to be repositioned – fast!

Why this works

- *"Senior managers like you"* is flattering but also repositions the call
- The objection handle roles seamlessly back into the call
- Demonstrates polite, directorial style control

"I'm in the middle of something right now!"

What client means

"I'm in the middle of something right now!" Although this statement could be a lie (just like *"He's in a meeting"*) we need to "accept" that this statement is true. As an objection it works for clients as salespeople normally go away, often not to return.

Average salesperson

Thinks: *"Liar! Everyone always tries to avoid me."*
Action: Tries to move ahead with the call thus creating resistance. Notably, this approach is likely to create resistance whether the client's initial statement was true or not.

"Sorry to have disturbed you. When would be more convenient to talk?
(Later in the week)
Thursday or Friday, which would be best for you?
(Friday)
Morning or afternoon?
(Morning)
10 or 11 am, which would you prefer?"

Sales Superstar

Thinks: *"OK. Then let's schedule a time that's more convenient for both of us."*
Understands: Treating this objection as true is the only professional option. The primary objective now is to schedule another call with the client. If the objection is a "lie" it may "disappear" during the scheduling process.

Why this works

- Respectful and courteous
- "Funnel" closes the client to an agreed time and date
- The only way out of this for the client is to give you the go ahead to talk to them now (i.e. *"What's the call regarding?"*)

"You need to speak to the human resources department."

What client means

"I see no value in speaking to you."
This client doesn't see the value in speaking with you and believes that this area of the business is / should be dealt with elsewhere.

Average salesperson

Thinks: *"Here we go again! Passed down to someone else like always."*
Action: Either departs "cap in hand" for the HR department or starts to "fight" this decision.

"I certainly will do that then, thank you. In order that I understand your business better and so that I can provide the best service to you through them tell me** (name client)**, what is the business advantage of working in that manner?"

Sales Superstar

Thinks: *"OK but now I'm here I'm going to get the most out of this call that I possibly can!"*
Understands: Many companies and decision-makers pass suppliers to non-decision making, non-outcome, orientated departments or individuals. Dealing with these departments is strategically important for long-term supplier partnerships but having a strong business relationship with key decision-makers is vital too.

Why this works

- Agrees to client's request
- Makes a clever statement which validates the need for the client to answer the question coming up
- Seeks out the key business needs and decision making strategies and starts a conversation

"I'm already talking to a couple of suppliers about this."

What client means

"I'm in purchasing mode but I've no time to waste."
This client believes that the chances are that you'll waste his time. With most salespeople he's probably right too! This comment will send all but the Sales Superstars into a bit of a desperate panic.

Average salesperson

Thinks: *"I can't believe I've missed another opportunity."*
Action: Either bails out of the call or becomes desperate neither of which will result in the opportunity to work with this client.

"Good. It's certainly important that any business decision such as this is researched properly and therefore that you're talking to the most compatible suppliers. Tell me, what were your business reasons for looking at *(the problem or the solution)* ***in the first place?*** *(Get answers)*

And that's exactly why... "

Sales Superstar

Thinks: *"Great! A hot lead. Bring it on!"*
Understands: This client is going to buy and has already completed the initial qualification process. To take a seat at the table the Sales Superstar must build rapid rapport, understand the client's business drivers and represent a credible option.

Why this works

- Demonstrates a strategic understanding of business relationships and needs
- Uncovers business drivers and links them to you and your solution

"Call back in 3 months."

What this means

"Get lost!"
Many clients, particularly people-orientated ones, have found that sounding interested and asking salespeople to call back is a great way of getting them off the line and avoiding any confrontation.

Average salesperson

Thinks: *"He like me but he has no need. I don't want to push too hard and upset him."*
Action: Ditches the call for fear of losing "the deal". Books a callback into the database and fills his "pipeline" with another weak call.

"Thanks for asking me to! At this point I guess most companies would schedule a call back for 3 months time. We at *(name company)* ***pride ourselves on working in partnership with our clients and I'd like to invest the time in meeting you now so that in 3 months time I'm in the best place to help you."***

Sales Superstar

Thinks: *"Not unless I have a real reason to pal!"*
Understands: This client needs qualifying before they're worthy of a callback. Nice people don't necessarily make the best clients!

Why this works

- Agrees with the client and is non-threatening
- Identifies that a "real" potential partner wouldn't just ring off and call back in 3 months time

"You've got two minutes."

What client means

"Please don't waste my time like that last idiot!" This client is trying to take control of the call and, what's more, on 95% of occasions will probably succeed. This time challenge is all too much for most "brow-beaten" salespeople!

Average salesperson

Thinks: *"I've interrupted him. He doesn't want to talk with me. I'd better hurry up."*
Action: Apologises for calling, rushes, mumbles, asks negative questions, expects to fail and does!

"Thank you. The reason for my call is..."

Sales Superstar

Thinks: *"That's all I need to get you wanting more!"*
Understands: People make a decision about you within seconds of speaking to you therefore this client will know within two minutes whether he wants to know more or not. First impressions count!

Why this works

- Acknowledges comment and takes control
- Is professional not emotional
- Delivery, pace and confidence imply seniority and importance

"I don't like you!"

What client means

"I don't like salespeople!"
Let's face it some clients are just down right rude at times! This client may be having a bad day or perhaps he's just obnoxious; in any case he's going to take it out on you!

Average salesperson

Thinks: *"I don't like me either!"*
Action: Feels bad, visualises a few negative memories, makes excuses and leaves the call.

"Then it's a good job I don't get emotional about building mutually beneficial business opportunities! The reason for my call is to..."

Sales Superstar

Thinks: *"Grow up!"*
Understands: This client doesn't even know you! Most salespeople will duck out of this call early on so what a great challenge for the Sales Superstar to turn it around!

Why this works

- Very tongue in cheek
- It reframes the situation and reminds the client of where they are (i.e. work!)
- It's professional and moves straight back to the call structure

"Send me literature."

What client means

"Go away!"
Clients have found that this is a really easy way to get rid of salespeople who are more than willing to send emails and literature because it gets them off the phone whilst they are doing it!

Average salesperson

Thinks: *"Yes, OK."*
Action: Takes the easy way out and misses an opportunity.

"I certainly will do that (and I'm pleased that you're interested in our company). As you may expect, we have a large amount of company literature. In order that it exactly meets your needs what I'd like to do is ask a few questions (come and meet with you) and from there I'll happily select the information which matches your needs."

Sales Superstar

Thinks: *"Most of my competitors will miss out here so this is a great opportunity."*
Understands: Literature at this stage would more than likely end up in the bin. Clients buy based on their problems, challenges and needs; failure to take the time to understand these buys only a ticket for a lottery!

Why this works

- Agrees with client's request
- Respects that he is busy
- Links to asking about him and his business

"What's the call regarding?"

What this client means

"Don't mess about pal!"
This is another unassuming phrase that sorts the wheat from the chaff as far as salespeople are concerned. By rights, it shouldn't be an objection but in practise it is!

Average salesperson

Thinks: *"He's onto me. He thinks that I'm a two-bob, second hand car dealer at heart!"*
Action: Feels pressurised and starts to blab about not wasting the client's time. Upshot? Wastes client's time!

"The reason for my call is to..."

Sales Superstar

Thinks: *"You asked for it!"*
Understands: This client just asked you what the call's regarding? Do you get a greener green light than that? Err ... no! Watch pace, tone, confidence and energy levels as you approach the call.

Why this works

- Confident and professional
- It's what the client asked for!
- It was never really an objection anyway!

"Why should I speak to you?"

What the client means

"I get a lot of sales calls. Don't waste my time." Clients know that this question puts all but the best salespeople onto the back foot. From the client's perspective it's very easy to take any answer that the salesperson gives and say that it's not a good enough reason to talk to them!

Average salesperson

Thinks: *"I don't know."*
Action: Desperately dumps heaps of information as fast as possible in the hope of hitting the mark! Too often they don't.

"You know that's a great question and there certainly are many business reasons why my clients do speak with me. Tell me, why wouldn't you speak to me?"

Sales Superstar

Thinks: *"I don't know yet but there are plenty of reasons so let's find them together!"*
Understands: Most clients don't really want a reason to talk, they want a reason not to! Our Sales Superstar will get underneath this objection and uncover the client's real needs and wants.

Why this works

- Acknowledges the client's question
- Links to *"business reasons"* and create credibility by mention of other *"clients"*
- Starts to uncover any real objections and / or drivers

"I'm not the right person."

What client means

"I'm not talking to you."
This is an interesting objection, as experience would suggest that this objection is often untrue. It is also irrefutable so it ends calls virtually instantaneously.

Average salesperson

Thinks: *"More duff info! Our database really is rubbish."*
Action: Asks who is the right person to talk to and exits the call thus missing an opportunity; not to mention going on what will probably be a "wild goose chase"!

Option 1: ***"At this point I guess most people would ask you who the decision maker is and hang up and call them but I believe that business is built on relationships and I would like to take the time to get to know you. Tell me..."***

Option 2: ***"Sorry about that, I thought that you were, my mistake. Who should I be speaking with? What is his / her role? What department is he / she in? What's the number? Thank you for all of your help. I wonder if you could help me a little more – tell me, what ...*** (move to whatever questions it would be useful for you to know).***"***

Sales Superstar

Thinks: *"I don't mind, I'm going to talk to you now we're speaking."*
Understands: This client could be lying or he could be telling the truth! Either way he could well hold the key to the puzzle of unlocking this account. A Sales Superstar aims to maximise his results from every sales call or visit.

Why this works

- Option 1 – most people are happy to say hello
- Option 2 - takes responsibility and uses misdirection
- Eventually the misdirection leads to information gathering questions

"I need more time to make a decision."

What client means

"There's something that I'm not telling you." This tactic is used a lot by clients who either aren't the only decision-maker, who find it hard to make decisions or have some kind of hidden objection. The problem from the salesperson's perspective is that once a deal starts to slow down they often stop altogether!

Average salesperson

Thinks: *"He doesn't want it! Is there a competitor sniffing around? Was it too expensive?"*
Action: Focuses on not losing a deal that hasn't even been won yet! Often cuts the price or offers a discount thus starting a price war or negotiation.

"Thanks for sharing that with me John. I'm happy to give you any information and answer any questions that you may have to help you to decide now. It's certainly important that you've made the right decision. Tell me John, what are the key factors upon which you are deciding?"

Sales Superstar

Thinks: *"I need to find out more about what you are deciding upon."*
Understands: A decision is not a static thing that just happens; a client needs to go through a "decision making process". A Sales Superstar becomes part of this process thus helping, influencing and coaching the client.

Why this works

- Demonstrates verbally that it is a process
- *"Decide now"* and *"you've made the right decision"* are both embedded commands
- The question starts to uncover the factors most important in the decision making process

"I haven't received it yet."

What client means

"I haven't received it yet!"
Not really an objection this one but it could be a stall for more time so it has to be dealt with. This only really works as an objection because of the emotional effect it has on some salespeople.

Average salesperson

Thinks: *"He's probably lying."*
Action: Feels irritated and sounds accusatory. Clearly, this doesn't lead to a great call.

"I'm sorry about that. Our literature is extensive anyway so what I'd like to do is tailor some specific information just for you and get it over to you right away. In order to do that what I need to do is ask a couple of questions. Tell me..."

Sales Superstar

Thinks: *"It doesn't matter. Talking about it is much better anyway."*
Understands: Early on in a relationship clients will rarely read generic literature. What's worse is that if they do, they will often prejudge whether they want to do business with you or not. Building strong client relationships and new business is about people not about paper!

Why this works

- Takes responsibility for the situation
- *"Right away"* implies urgency
- Links to needs based questions

"I need to speak with other decision-makers."

What client means

"I need more time to decide" or *"I lied to you about being the decision maker."*
This is a pretty good objection for clients, as salespeople just don't know what to say to it. If it is true then what can you do? If it's not how can you call the client a liar?!

Average salesperson

Thinks: *"Liar! Liar! Pants are on fire!"*
Action: Tries to push to expose or pressurise the client. Whilst this will occasionally work its clearly not a great strategy!

"That's fine. It's certainly crucial that an important investment like this one is fully supported. In order that I can give you all of the support you need and answer any questions they may have I'd like to ask a few questions. Tell me, how many other..."

Sales Superstar

Thinks: *"How do I get this moving again?"*
Understands: Whatever the truth is here the important thing is to rebuild rapport, regain trust and agree a way forward. If there's a hidden objection the Sales Superstar will find it.

Why this works

- Respects the client's position and reframes thinking to *"important investment"*
- Everyone likes *"support"* if offered correctly
- Questions about the others involved "smokes out" hidden objections and decision-making strategies
- If it's true that there are other decision-makers then you can start to construct an action plan

"Call me at the end of the week."

What client means

"Go away for now."
This client is either too busy to talk right now and wants to talk to you later in the week or they are hopeful that they will be able to avoid you in the future. There could well be a hidden objection here.

Average salesperson

Thinks: *"Yes. OK."*
Action: Agrees to call back and exits the call leaving control of the relationship firmly in the hands of the client.

***"Thanks for asking me to. When in the week would be best for you? Thursday or Friday**?*
AM or PM, which would be best?
3 or 4 PM?"
*(*And then confirm call time to client)

Sales superstar

Thinks: *"You're not getting away that easily!"*
Understands: Average salespeople handicap their potential with unqualified and irrelevant leads. Working this unpromising pipeline restricts the time that they have available for identifying quality clients.

Why this works

- Sets up a qualified call worthy of your pipeline
- 95% of clients will ask you what the call's regarding allowing you to continue the call now with their permission

"Are you serious?"

What client means

"Not another sales call!"
This objection is nothing more than "bluster" and has no real substance. Ironically, emotionally based objections are often amongst the most challenging for sales people having a bad day!

Average salesperson

Thinks: *"No, I'm worthless. Why do I bother with this job?"*
Actions: Becomes defensive, verging on the aggressive. Needless to say – the call's going nowhere fast!

"Yes, I am."

(Takes a breath for impact and then continues with call).

Sales Superstar

Thinks: *"Yes. Totally."*
Understands: Clients can't buy off every salesperson they meet as no client could possibly have that many needs. Most salespeople will back off at this type of objection. Ignoring it will put our Sales Superstar in the top 10% of salespeople before they even start selling!

Why this works

- Answers the question
- Psychologically takes control and passes the message that this call is important enough to take seriously
- Moves elegantly back to your planned call structure

"You can't help me!"

What client means

"I don't want to speak with you."
This client has made a decision not to speak to you based purely upon the fact that you are a salesperson.

Average salesperson

Thinks: *"Why is everyone I call so rude?"*
Action: Feels rejected (again), pitches his product desperately and ends up reinforcing the client's original opinion.

"Oh, I'm sorry! Many of my other clients thought that too before they saw the benefits of what we do. I'm sure you have good reasons for saying that – do you mind me asking what they are?"

Sales Superstar

Thinks: *"How can I turn this around?"*
Understands: This client is only objecting to the sales call in general not to you personally. Once you've built professional rapport this objection will probably disappear.

Why this works

- The apology takes ownership and is unexpected
- Breaking the client's pattern here is important
- It acknowledges that the client has reasons for his opinion
- The question then starts a conversation and digs for any real objections

"I'll take it if you discount!"

What client means

"I think I can get a deal here!"
In this situation the client thinks that they have the upper hand. Past experience will lead them to believe that salespeople will always discount to get the deal.

Average salesperson

Thinks: *"Oh, please don't let me lose it now!"*
Action: Starts to worry and allows the fear of loss to cloud his better judgement and negotiating skills.

"I'm pleased that you have made your decision and I understand that return on investment is important to you, however you have secured our best discount already. When are you looking to receive the product / get started?"

Sales Superstar

Thinks: *"I know you want it anyway!"*
Understands: This client wants the product or solution and this is an attempt to do a deal. Chances are that this is not a serious negotiation. If it is then it's the Sales Superstar's job to help the client to attach more value to the investment.

Why this works

- *"Decision"* implies something that is decided already
- *"Secured"* is an ego-flattering word
- Moves to a question which, if answered, presupposes the deal is done
- If the client is serious about negotiating then this is a "strong" starting position

"Is this negotiable?"

What client means

"Have I got the best price?"
Clients have found that this seemingly unassuming question sends many salespeople into free-fall offering silly discounts! Wouldn't you try it if it worked most times too?

Average salesperson

Thinks: *"Oh no! I can't lose it now! How much can I discount this by?"*
Action: Moves into negotiations too quickly or even worse offers a huge discount. Ironically, this can lose the deal altogether due to the unstated message to the client about the low value of the product / service or the perception that the original price was too high.

"Yes, of course it is. How much more do you want to pay?

(Client laughs or sounds shocked – breaking their pattern. Now slow down and speak genuinely...)

No, seriously ... you have already secured our best discount. When would you be looking to accept delivery?"

Sales Superstar

Thinks: *"Not likely. It's worth every penny!"*
Understands: This client wants to buy and is now discussing terms. The balance of power has changed. It's up to the Sales Superstar to maintain the value of the proposition.

Why this works

- Answers the question and breaks the "let's negotiate" pattern by injecting humour
- Uncovers the times when you do have to negotiate for real
- Moves to a close using the presupposition that the deal is done

"How long will this proposed meeting take?"

Client means

"Maybe but I'm not sure."
This client has not made up their mind about having a meeting with you yet and is going to make their decision based upon your response.

Average salesperson

Thinks: *"I can't believe it! Just when I thought I'd got it!"*
Action: Makes excuses, downgrades the importance of the meeting by reducing the time needed, talks rubbish and blows the meeting!

"That's a great question and I understand that we both need to get maximum benefit from the meeting. In order to do that, I estimate that the meeting will take about an hour depending upon how many questions that you have for me. Tell me, who else *(is there anyone else)* ***within your organisation*** *(who)* ***may benefit from taking part in this meeting?"***

Sales Superstar

Thinks: *"See you at the meeting!"*
Understands: This client sees the value in a meeting but needs confirmation that you won't be wasting their time. This is done through the psychological message (tone, pace, pitch, timbre etc.) not through verbal persuasion.

Why this works

- Acknowledges that both parties need to get maximum benefit from the meeting (this puts you on your client's level)
- Psychologically appears to put responsibility for the timing of the meeting into your client's hands
- In answering the *"who else"* question the client accepts that the meeting is taking place

"We're not reviewing our suppliers at the moment. Can you send some literature so that we can consider you next time?"

What client means

"Not for you anyway! Go away!"
Most clients are keen to get you into their "process" for approval as it gets you off the phone in exchange for the future promise of consideration for supply! Once this "consideration" is given, most average salespeople are too scared to push any more for fear of it reflecting badly on their chances of selection!

Average salesperson

Thinks: *"I'll find out when they are due to review their suppliers, send some literature and call back then."*
Action: Takes time and effort preparing paperwork and calling back – usually pointless.

"That's fine because I wouldn't ask you to change now as I understand that forming strong supplier relationships is all about long term partnerships, profitability and return on investment. I believe that business is built on relationships and I would still like to invest the time now in getting to know and you and your business. Tell me..."

Sales Superstar

Thinks: *"But you might be soon!"*
Understands: Clients review their suppliers all of the time and are often economic with the truth about the "real" processes. Clients also regularly buy from outside of their listed suppliers to meet specific needs.

Why this works

- Agrees with the client position
- Demonstrates your understanding of business partnerships at a decision making level
- Very few people don't want to get to know you
- Ignores second objection about sending literature altogether!

"You're not big enough. We only deal with larger suppliers!"

What client means

"I don't want to know. Go away!"
This objection works wonders for clients as the hidden put down *("we only work with larger suppliers")* strikes straight to the ego of most salespeople. Also, it may well be true that they do have such a policy.

Average salesperson

Thinks: *"Why do I work for such a useless company?"*
Actions:
1) Bails out of the call feeling bad and adding to his negativity, or
2) Becomes defensive and starts to "argue" with the client as to why he should use him!

"It's certainly true that we're not the largest supplier in the market place although we do work with many of the key players such as** ... (name clients)**. Tell me,** (name client)**, what's important to you about dealing with large suppliers?"

Sales Superstar

Thinks: *"Then it's my job to help you to understand the benefits of working with a smaller supplier!"*
Understands: This objection is probably just an excuse. If it is a real objection the Sales Superstar needs to uncover the factors that helped the client to come to this decision in the first place. By understanding these factors he will be able to help the client to reassess that process and potentially come to a different decision.

Why this works

- Agrees with the client's position and makes a power statement about his own clients
- Positive language *"not the largest supplier"* is psychologically better than "small"!
- "*What's important?"* digs out the original deciding factors and enables the Sales Superstar to reposition his solution to match them

Six Simple Strategies That Will Handle Any Objection!

Strategy 1 - Don't Fan Fires!

When I was a young lad I used to love going on school camp. One of the most exciting things about camp was getting to cook your own food on an open flame. I remember the first time we had a go at it and we built this massive fire to cook our fantastic feast on. Unfortunately, all we managed to do was incinerate the bacon and eggs within seconds!

One of the teachers came over to us and explained that it was all about controlling the flames not stoking them up!

When I run seminars and programmes I am constantly amazed by how even quite senior salespeople manage to fan really quite minor objections into raging infernos with a combination of their own perceptions, emotions and reactions. <u>When you take the time to control your emotions and reaction you can really start to control the fire.</u>

With cold calling in particular many of the opening objections given by clients are merely bluster and have no substance behind them whatsoever. Even when they do have some substance (e.g. *"we use another supplier"*) they don't necessarily require an answer right away. Acknowledging the objection and moving on is sometimes all that is required at this stage.

Unless there is any particular reason why, I will normally approach most first objections in a cold call in this manner!

Objections:

"We have no budget..."
"We have no need..."
"We use another supplier..."
"We have a preferred supplier's list..."
"It's nearly the end of the financial year..."
"It's not my decision..."
"I need to speak to someone else..."

Answer:

"***That's fine***. *The reason for my call is to..."*

Or, and if you really must say more...

"***That's fine. I wouldn't expect it to be any other way***. *The reason for my call is to..."*

Strategy 2 – People Buy People So *Sell on Relationships!*

People buy people. If everything else were equal wouldn't you buy from the person that you liked the best? Of course you would and so do your clients. This may seem obvious but it is a fact that's often overlooked by most salespeople. This is a shame because it's a fact that we can use to great advantage when selling.

Most clients are worried that you are going to push something onto them that they don't want. Why? Because we've all experienced salespeople in our lives who do this. By focusing on the relationship and not on the sale you start to put your clients more at ease. This allows them to stop worrying that they are about to get "pitched".

When I teach this simple technique to delegates and they get on the phones and try it they are always amazed at just how effective it really is.

Objections:

"We've got no need..."
"We've got no budget..."
"It's the end of the financial year..."
"It's not my decision..."
"You need to speak to someone else..."

The "Building Relationships" Answer:

"That's fine. At this point most of my competitors would ask you when you do have a budget and arrange to call you back then. We at *... (name company)* ***... believe that business is built on relationships and I would still like to invest the time in getting to know you now. Tell me John, how...?"***

Strategy 3 – People Like to Be Complemented

This principle is a little similar to the last approach and is based on the fact that most clients expect you to confront their objections, head on. By using this approach you avoid any confrontation and disarm your client because it is not what he is expecting. Importantly, you also differentiate yourself from the competition.

Objections:

"We have an existing supplier…"
"We use in-house solutions…"
"We farm that out to the states…"
"We have an internal person in charge of that area…"
"We use your competitors (ABC etc)…"

Answer:

"That's fine. I wouldn't expect it to be any other way. Many of my other clients said that before they became aware of how what we do complements what they are already doing. What I'd like to do is come down and see you / ask a couple of questions…"

Strategy 4 – Feel, Felt, Found

***"I understand the way that you feel.
Other people felt that way too.
What they found was that..."***

(Write your own feel, felt, found with a real case study in the space below...)

Strategy 5 – Respect People's Reasons

When I am selling I know that the majority of people who have a need for my services will already be getting something similar somewhere else. They will also have gone to some time and effort to find and select their current suppliers. Depending on the product I am selling, changing suppliers may be really quite difficult for the client in terms of time, logistics, cost, related systems etc. Clients are not sitting around waiting for a call from me so that they can change suppliers when I call them!

In fact, I don't want it to be that easy at all! If it was, anybody could call my clients and get an opportunity! I don't want clients that give everything out to anybody who rings them! I want clients with whom I can build meaningful and long-lasting business relationships.

It always amazes me that most salespeople want to turn around these kinds of objections with just one call. It shows a total lack of understanding of the client, their needs, or indeed of how clients really use our products. What kind of message does this kind of behaviour send to your clients about your business awareness?

<u>The way to deal with this kind of situation is to take the time to understand your client's reasons and situation more fully.</u>

Objections:

"We have existing suppliers..."
"We have preferred supplier's list..."
"We do this in-house..."
"We contract this out..."
"This is controlled by the US..."

Answer:

"Thanks for sharing that with me and I wouldn't expect it to be any other way (I'm pleased that you take this area of your business so seriously). I'm sure that you had good business reasons for putting that in place. Do you mind me asking, what were they?"

(And ask as if you mean to get an answer!)

Strategy 6 - Stepping Stones

Clients tell you what you need to know. Their words are like cement and you are the water. The question is ... Are you going to build a stepping stone or a weight to drown yourself with?

With stepping stones we leverage the client's own words to create a platform from which we can move towards our desired outcome. This is particularly effective when setting meetings but can be used in many ways. Read the examples below and then read **"Real Conversations"** for more detailed examples of Stepping Stones.

What is a Stepping-Stone?

Your questions
+ client answer
+ ***"that's exactly why..."***
+ ***because".***

You can use this pretty much anywhere, see opposite...

Example 1:

You: *"I'm sure that you have good reasons for not doing sales training. Do you mind me asking, what were they?"*

Client: *"Well, it's too expensive and last time I didn't get results."*

You: *"John, I can see that would create questions and queries <u>and that's exactly why</u> we need to meet."* (Close)

Example 2:

You: *"I'd still like to invest in getting to know you. Tell me John, what size team do you have down there?"*

Client: *"Oh, about 60."*

You: *"How many of them are involved face to face with clients?"*

Client: *"Most of them I guess."*

You: *"You know <u>that's exactly why</u> we need to meet <u>because</u>..."* (Note in this example that the word because is about to link to reasons why the meeting would be good.)

Example 3:

Client: *"I've heard bad stuff about your industry. It's too expensive."*

You: *"I've heard that said too but it really doesn't reflect the return on investment that many of our clients have been getting <u>and that's exactly why</u> we need to meet..."*

Real Conversations

Real Conversations

These three conversations are excerpts from conversations that my delegates have had after training. Most of the conversations that I have chosen are ones where they were closing for a meeting. This is because they have no industry specific questions in them and are therefore applicable to any sales situation. It is a simple matter to close in the same manner to the next set of questions...

Conversation 1: The Easy One!

Sales: *"... I'm sure there may be areas in which we can work together. In order to find out what benefits we may be able to add what I'd like to do is come and see you..."*

Client: *"Is this a cold call?"* (Emotional objection)

Sales: *"Yes. The reason for my call is to introduce myself and my organisation and to set up a meeting with you."* (Answers with a simple "Yes" and moves on).

Client: *"Can't you send me literature first?"* (Standard client response)

Sales: *"Yes, I certainly can send you literature first. However, our literature is pretty generic so what I'd rather do is come down and see you and then I can tailor the literature to suit your exact* *needs."* (Derivation of standard literature approach)

Client: *"I'm really not sure. I'm quite busy at the moment."* (Thinking about the meeting)

Sales: *"That's fine John. I'm quite busy too. I wasn't thinking for at least 4-6 weeks. How's your diary looking at the end of January, say the 24th or the 25th. Which would be better for you?"*
(Acknowledges objection and picks up on the *"at the moment"* comment by positioning himself as busy too. Moves straight to an alternative close in the future)

Client: *"Hmm. Neither of those are that good."* (By implication, the client is now accepting the meeting, just not on these dates)

Sales: *"When would be better then?"* (Open question)

Client: *"The following week I guess, towards the end?"*

Sales: *"Thursday or Friday John?"*

Client: *"Friday."*

Salesperson sets up the meeting.

Conversation 2: No Need!

Client: *"Can I stop you there. We have no need for sales coaching at the moment."*

Sales: *"That's fine. The reason for the call was purely to introduce myself and my company and to organise a meeting with you. What we do is work with companies like yours to help them to increase sales and maximise profitability. I'm sure that there are areas where we may be able to help you. In order to do that what I'd like to do is come and see you."* (Answered simply with *"that's fine"* and then moved back to the planned suggestion of a meeting*)*

Client*: "I just don't have the time at the moment."* (Standard time objection again)

Sales: *"John, I won't waste a moment of your time. I'm very busy too so I was thinking towards the end of January. How's the 24th or 25th looking to you?"* (Simple answer, agrees that they're both busy, links to a slightly different diary close)

Client: *"Well that would be alright but I just don't see the need at this time."* (A ha! Client has nominally agreed to the meeting but the *"need"* objection has come back)

Sales: *"That's fine. Many of my competitors would ask you when you are going to have a need and arrange to call you then. I believe that business is* *built on relationships and I'd still like to invest the time in getting to know you. Which of those two dates would you prefer, the 24th or the 25th?"* (Agrees and then uses the stock *"relationships"* approach. Closes straight out on the two dates as the client has already nominally agreed to them)

Client: *"Probably the 24th. Is this going to take a long time?"* (Client agreeing to the meeting but still wriggling a bit. His real concern here is not the meeting but the potential that it may go on too long!)

Sales: *"No, it won't. To get the most value from the meeting I expect about an hour but that really depends on how many questions that you have for me. What time on the 24th would be best?"* (Answers with a simple *"No"*, introduces the value concept and then throws the responsibility to the client by linking the length of the meeting to how many questions the client has. Closes to a specific time on the 24th!)

Client: *"Well about 4pm I think but I really don't have a need at this time."* (One final check that he won't be bullied!)

Sales: *"That's fine John. See you on the 24th at 4pm."* (Chooses to confirm meeting confidently having judged that this would be enough to reassure the client)

Closes off with meeting!

Conversation 3: The Existing Supplier

Client: *"I think that I had better stop you there. I am totally happy with my current suppliers."*

Sales: *"That's fine. The reason for the call was merely to set up a meeting to explore areas of mutual interest. How's your diary looking towards the back end of January, say the 24th or the 25th? Which would be better for you?"* (Bearing in mind that the objection was not even a question all the salesperson has to do is acknowledge and close)

Client: *"Well, I'm always busy but I just don't see any point in getting together as I'm not looking to change suppliers?"*

Sales: *"That's fine. I'm not asking you to change now merely have a look at what we're involved with. We've worked with several of the major players in the market place to help them to increase revenues and maximise profitability. Like you, I'm very busy. I'm sure that there would be some mutual benefit in getting together. When you look at those days, which would be the more suitable, the 24th or the 25th?"* (Acknowledges again but this time gives a bit more. Note the embedded commands and the controlled close "*when you look at those days*")

Client: *"The 24th but I don't see any point. I'm happy with my suppliers. I really don't want to change."*

Sales: *"John, I'm not asking you to change, merely to agree to a meeting. Building the correct supplier relationships is essential to any business and I'm sure that you had great reasons for working with your current suppliers. Do you mind me asking, what were they?"* (Agrees again, uses a link statement and then moves to understanding the situation better. Note this is the start of using a Stepping Stone)

Client: *"No, of course not. We used to use a lot of suppliers but we found that we were not getting the levels of service that we needed. We need to be able to control our suppliers and get maximum benefits from them."*

Sales: *"Service is certainly an important aspect of any relationship – what are the critical elements that you look for?"* (Questioning to understand)

Client: *"Our operation down here is massive. We have 5 sites and 1000 employees. We're shipping kit out at least twice a day. Some of our clients need to be able to phone up, order and receive delivery within 48 hours. We can't hold enough stock to do this so we need a fast and reliable service from our suppliers."* (Stating needs now)

Sales: *"Sounds like you're pretty busy down there. How much stock are you ordering in a typical week then?"* (Pacing and leading)

Client: *"It all depends, several thousand pieces. It's a handful for any supplier."* (A ha!)

Sales: *"I suppose that it must be. What kind of challenges do you get?"* (Not leaping in too fast!)

Client: *"Not a lot but when they do occur it's mostly just around the fact that it's difficult for any one supplier to cover the changes in our stock usage."*

Sales: *"John, that's exactly why I'd like to come and see you because we've worked with several of your competitors in helping them to secure a fast and reliable service with total flexibility. I'm sure what we do could really complement your existing suppliers as regards to your changing stock usage. What time on the 24th would be the best for you?"* (Uses the Stepping Stone and links the *"because"* to the client's own needs and in his own words. Clever use of *"complements"* too and then a simple close)

Client: *"Oh, I guess sometime in the morning."*

Closes out for the meeting.

Conclusion

"Thanks for taking the time to study **Objections! Objections! Objections**! I am confident that you will have enjoyed it and hope that you implement new strategies and techniques, win more sales and move closer towards your dreams and goals. I would be delighted to hear of your wins and successes.

As a valued customer I also appreciate your feedback so please let me know your thoughts, musings, comments and anything that you would love to see covered in future products and programmes. I would also be keen to hear of any new or specialist objections that you struggle with!

And remember – go out and sell with attitude!"

Gavin

If you want to know more about Gavin and why he is considered by many to be the leading expert in maximising sales performance under intense competition in the UK today then visit www.gaviningham.net now. Focused on the core sales challenges of fear of selling, fear of rejection, fear of cold calling and staying motivated can you afford not to?

Now is the time to...

Explode the performance of your business through sales coaching, training and consultancy

Book an inspiring and uplifting keynote for your next conference or AGM

Focus on development through cutting edge learning products

Breakthrough with one to one coaching for the incredibly committed peak performer

Gavin Ingham Ltd
0870 011 7864
info@gaviningham.net
www.gaviningham.net